LEONA MITCHELL
OPERA STAR

GWENDOLYN HOOKS

I AM OKLAHOMA
CHILDREN'S SERIES

SERIES EDITOR: GINI MOORE CAMPBELL

OKLAHOMA HALL *of* FAME
OKLAHOMA HERITAGE ASSOCIATION PUBLISHING

OKLAHOMA HALL *of* FAME

2015 OFFICERS AND DIRECTORS

Unless otherwise noted, photos courtesy of the Oklahoma Hall of Fame.
Cover photo courtesy Yousef Khanfar.

©2015 Oklahoma Heritage Association Publishing, a publication of the Oklahoma Hall of Fame

Printed in Canada
ISBN: 978-1-938923-22-7
LIBRARY OF CONGRESS CONTROL NUMBER: 2015948200

Book and Cover Design: Skip McKinstry

LEONA MITCHELL
OPERA STAR

Chapter I   Oklahoma's Cultural Ambassador

Leona Mitchell is an opera singer. Opera is like a play. But no one talks. Everyone sings their parts. Leona's voice made her famous. She sang for princes and kings. She sang for **ambassadors**. Four presidents of the United States asked her to sing for them. She sang around the world.

There are 365 days in a year. Every year, Leona sang 300 days. She did this for 30 years. Opera critics said her voice gleamed. Opera critics watch operas. Then they write about how well the singers performed. Another critic said Leona sang gloriously. Full of drama!

Oklahomans are proud of Leona. She rode on the Oklahoma Rising float in Macy's Thanksgiving Day Parade in New York City.

At home in Enid, Oklahoma, the city named two streets after her. One is Leona Mitchell Boulevard. The other is Leona Mitchell Place.

She has won many awards. Leona Mitchell is Oklahoma's opera star.

In 2004, Oklahoma Governor Brad Henry named Leona Mitchell an Oklahoma Cultural Ambassador. *Courtesy Yousef Khanfar.*

Yousef Khanfar

Chapter 2   The Musical Mitchells

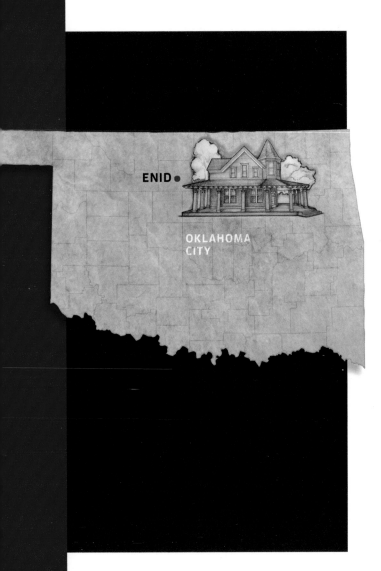

ENID •

OKLAHOMA
CITY

Leona was born on October 13, 1949. Her father, Hulon, pastored the Antioch Church of God in Christ. He sang and played instruments. Her mother, Pearl, was a nurse. She was a piano teacher, too.

Leona had 14 brothers and sisters. They sang and played instruments. Leona played the violin and piano.

The family formed a **gospel** music group. They were The Musical Mitchells. They sang all over Oklahoma and Kansas. They also sang in Missouri and Texas. They even sang on national television.

Leona Mitchell was inducted into the Oklahoma Hall of Fame on November 18, 2004. Induction is the highest honor an Oklahoman can receive from the state. She was presented for induction by Tom J. McDaniel.

It was on a talent show. It was the *Ted Mack Original Amateur Hour*. People all over the United States gathered around their televisions to watch it.

Leona loved to sing. But her brothers teased her. One brother said she could not sing her way out of a paper bag. She did not listen. She kept singing.

She had many friends. Leona invited them home for sleepovers. There was always room for one more at the Mitchell house.

Leona's parents encouraged her to work hard in school. She loved history. She loved learning French and Spanish. She planned to be a **linguist** or **diplomat** when she grew up.

In high school, Leona enrolled in choir. Maureen Priebe was **choir director**. On her first day, the class stood up and sang together. First, Mrs. Priebe asked one student to sit down. Then she asked another student to sit down. Whose beautiful voice did she hear? Soon only one student was standing.

It was Leona!

Chapter 3   Hello Opera

"Once I heard Leona sing, I had a whole new appreciation for opera. I fell in love with her voice. I moved to Oklahoma City from my home in Detroit to study opera at Oklahoma City University just like she did."
DEONNA CATTLEDGE, OPERA STUDENT.

Leona's voice was powerful. She out-sang the others. Mrs. Priebe loaned Leona opera records. It was the first time Leona had heard opera. "They sing so high," she thought. "They sing like birds." She tried singing it. Leona could sing like the ladies on the records! Her voice soared from high notes to low notes. Her voice bounced back from walls.

For three years, Mrs. Priebe worked with Leona. They sang before school. They sang after school. During her senior year, Mrs. Priebe

Leona was very active at Oklahoma City University. She was honored by the National Association of Teachers of Singing.
Courtesy Oklahoma City University.

thought Leona should sing in college. She asked Leona to **audition** at Oklahoma City University.

Leona practiced an **aria** for her audition. The song was from the Italian opera *Aida*. She did not know Italian. Mrs. Priebe helped her. She taught her to sing it phonetically. That meant she learned how to imitate the sounds of the words she heard on the records.

Mrs. Priebe drove Leona to Oklahoma City for her audition. The judges stopped the students after they sang a minute or two. But they listened to Leona for 15 minutes! The judges rushed into the room. They said she must study with them. They knew her parents had 15 children. The judges would find college money for her. They gave her a four-year **scholarship**. It was the first voice scholarship they had ever offered to a student!

Both Leontyne Price and Maria Callas were sopranos like Leona. After Leona began singing professionally, she and Leontyne became friends.

Chapter 4   Off to See the World

At college, Leona learned that most operas are written in Italian, French, or German. Leona studied Spanish in junior high school. She studied French in high school. She had to learn the others.

One summer, she won a singing contest. She used her winnings to take music classes. She signed up for Opera in the Ozarks. Leona made sure she got to Inspiration Point, Arkansas, because it was one of the best music camps in the United States.

Leona won the lead in the *Ballad of Baby Doe*. During rehearsals, she was upset because she had to wear a white wig. *Courtesy Oklahoma City University Archives.*

"There were other college classes, and acting lessons, and diction lessons, and dance lessons, and foreign languages, and making tapes, and memorizing roles, and listening to records—because opera is not just singing." Leona Mitchell

When summer was over, Leona headed back to college. She sang in the opera, *Ballad of Baby Doe*. It was set in Colorado during the wild silver mining days. Leona played Baby Doe. A few months later, she played Rosalina in *Die Fledermaus* (The Bat).

While she was in college, Leona won many awards and scholarships. She auditioned for the Merola Award. Hundreds of people applied. Only 20 students would win. She was one of them. Leona graduated from college in 1971. She earned a Bachelor of Arts in Music degree. She moved to San Francisco, California, a long way from Oklahoma.

Leona was off to see the world.

Leona was a member of the Madrigal Singers. The group performed across the Oklahoma City community. Leona is in the top row, second from right. *Courtesy Oklahoma City University Archives*

Chapter 5 From San Francisco to New York City

At Merola, in San Francisco, Leona learned what makes a successful opera. She learned from **professional** singers. **Voice coaches** improved her voice. Directors and **orchestra conductors** explained their roles. She learned how to move on stage. Act. Breathe. Some operas have fight scenes. It is stage combat. She learned to use knives and swords.

Leona worked hard. Merola was a place where dreams come true. Other opera singers started their careers there. Leona was determined to do it, too.

She got her chance one evening in 1972. Leona waited backstage at the San Francisco War Memorial Opera House. It would be her first time singing as a professional.

The lights dimmed. A hush spread over the audience. The conductor raised his **baton**. The orchestra answered with the music of *Carmen*. The music spread across the 3,000-seat auditorium. Leona took a deep breath. She became Micaela. She was a faithful village girl. But she lost her soldier boyfriend to a gypsy. Her singing and acting made the audience believe she really was Micaela. The opera world noticed her performance.

Most opera singers begin their careers in small opera houses in Europe. Then big opera houses, like the New York Metropolitan Opera (Met), cast them in roles. Not Leona.

She studied for a year at The Juilliard School in New York City. Word spread about the amazing singer from Oklahoma. The Met asked her to sing the role of Micaela.

She did that in San Francisco. Leona was nervous. Could she do it again?

At Merola in San Francisco, California, Leona won the James Schwabacher Memorial Award. Her work there was the beginning of a fantastic career.

She would sing with the famous Spanish singer, Placido Domingo. He was one of The Three Tenors. Placido and two other tenors were the best in the world.

Leona's career was just beginning. Would it end that night? Was she too young? To sing with Placido was exciting. It was also scary. She did not want to fail.

Leona should not have worried. She was sensational. The Met asked her to sing in *The Magic Flute* and *La Boheme* (artists).

Leona became the first Oklahoman to sing at the Met. She sang there for 18 years!

Chapter 6   A Voice for Thousands

Leona had a strong voice. Sometimes she sang in auditoriums with 5,000 seats. Without a microphone! People in the last row could easily hear her.

Leona began as a **lyric soprano**. She could sing high notes. Then she became a **spinto soprano**. She could also sing deep, dark, dramatic tones. She could blast her voice like a trumpet.

In 1976, Leona heard a record company planned to record an opera. The opera was *Porgy and Bess*. She auditioned for a small part. She wanted to sing the song, "Summertime". The producer loved her voice. She won the lead role of Bess.

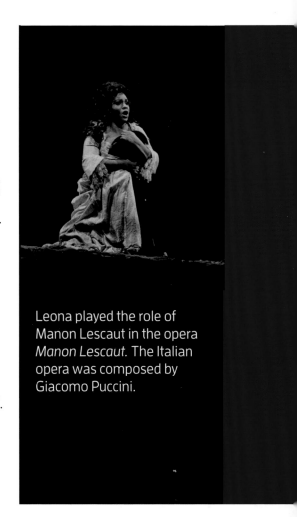

Leona played the role of Manon Lescaut in the opera *Manon Lescaut*. The Italian opera was composed by Giacomo Puccini.

"Work hard and take the lumps," is Leona's advice to aspiring opera singers

Leona in *Aida* at The Metropolitan Opera in 1988. Aida was one of her favorite roles. *Courtesy The Metropolitan Opera Archives.*

Porgy and Bess was an African American opera. It takes place in the early 1900's. It was set in the small community called Catfish Row, South Carolina.

Leona sang from her heart. She sang as if Catfish Row was her true home. She won a Grammy Award. It is an award for outstanding work in the music business.

The role of Bess made Leona an international success. She sang in opera houses in Paris, London, Rome, Sydney, Buenos Aires, Egypt, and more.

Chapter 7   Under the Egyptian Stars

One of her most exciting adventures happened in Egypt. She would sing in the opera *Aida*. It takes place in Egypt during the times of **Pharaohs**. A stage was built outdoors. **Ancient pyramids** stood in the background. Leona transformed herself into Aida. She sang under the stars. She transported audiences to a time long ago. Her voice thrilled them.

In 1983, Leona sang in the opera *Ernani*. She would sing with another of The Three Tenors. It was Italian singer Luciano Pavarotti. Pavarotti played Ernani. Leona was Elvira. Ernani loved Elvira. But Elvira was engaged to the King. *The New York Times* said Pavarotti was on fire. They said Leona's voice soared.

A few years later, Leona sang with the third of The Three Tenors. He was the Spanish singer, Jose Carreras. They sang together in *Carmen*.

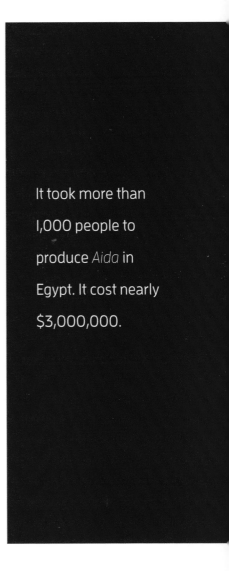

It took more than 1,000 people to produce *Aida* in Egypt. It cost nearly $3,000,000.

"I really want to go wherever my voice is leading me."
Leona Mitchell

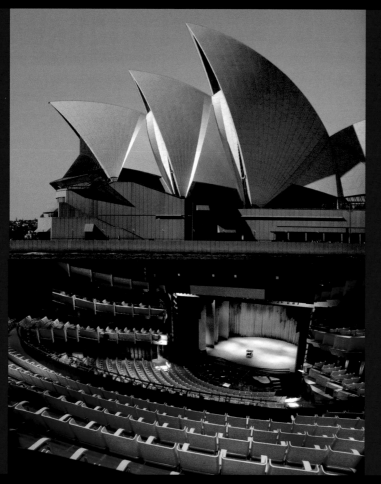

Leona performed many times at the Sydney Opera. The opera house is located in Sydney, Australia. It is one of the most recognized buildings on earth.
Courtesy Sydney Opera.

Leona performed from this stage at the Sydney Opera. It is the Joan Sutherland Theatre.
Courtesy Sydney Opera.

Leona delighted the audience at the Santa Fe Opera in the *Marriage of Figaro* in 1976. *Courtesy Santa Fe Opera.*

"Leona was so personal that it was easy to forget that she's a world-wide celebrity. We had a nice Oklahoma-style chat. And then I went to her concert, and WHAM—her talent came pouring out! Even my family members, who are not opera fans, were brought to tears by the beauty and emotion of her voice."

AMY DEE STEPHENS,
OKLAHOMA CITY
JOURNALIST

Leona in *Madam Butterfly*. It was composed by Giacomo Puccini. It is one of the most performed operas.
Courtesy Metropolitan Opera Archives.

Chapter 8   Tales of Disappointment

Leona was successful. But sometimes she felt unsure of herself. She had stage fright. She wanted to quit. One night, she watched a television show. An entertainer talked about feeling the same way. He overcame it. Inspired, Leona regained her confidence. She continued to delight audiences all over the world.

Singers audition for roles. They hope they get it. They might not. Mostly, Leona got her roles. But not always. One musical director said no. She could not sing the role of Donna Anna in the Italian opera *Don Giovanni*. It was because she was African American.

Another time, a director said no. He did not want her to sing in the French opera, *Tales of Hoffman*. Again it was because of her race. Her manager said he would tell the public.

The director backed down. Leona got the role.

Leona missed her induction into the Oklahoma Women's Hall of Fame because she was under contract to sing at the Met. She signed the contract four years earlier. Luckily, her parents were able to attend and accept her award

Chapter 9   Such a Lot of World to See

Many of Leona's fans write to her. They write about their pain and troubles. They tell how she comforts them. Her voice transports them to a different world. Her mother was right. She always told Leona music was not just a career, it was her purpose in life.

She traveled with her husband, Elmer Coles Bush III. Their son, Elmer IV, traveled with them, too. Sometimes he was homeschooled. Other times he went to school. It depended on how long they would be in one place. He attended school with Australian kids. He also went to school with New York City kids.

Little Elmer loved music. He practiced conducting with his baton. Once, when he was two years old he stood near the stage. His mother was singing. But the audience watched him conduct. His father had to whisk him away.

"You must have tenacity—develop the hide of an elephant."
Leona Mitchell.

Leona's powerful voice continues to win her fans. She travels, sings, and teaches classes showing students what they can accomplish with hard work and determination.

Back in Enid, her mother would call and ask, "When will we get to see you?" Leona was busy singing. She did not take vacations. It was hard to visit family.

Sometimes she felt like an outsider. It was as if she looked at family gatherings through a window. Telephone calls were not fun. She could not talk long. Her voice had to rest.

But Leona returned to Oklahoma as often as she could. She invited her family to travel with her. Brothers, sisters, nieces, and nephews traveled with her to other countries.

Leona believes in helping others. She wants to be like Mrs. Priebe. Every summer, Leona has a music camp. It is for girls and boys who like to sing. She hopes they will understand the beauty of opera.

Since she was a little girl, Leona has sung for thousands. Music lovers still rush to hear her voice. She likes to tell the story of growing up in Oklahoma. No matter how far she travels, she carries Oklahoma in her heart. Leona is a perfect Oklahoma Cultural Ambassador.

People use special words when they have enjoyed an opera. If they love a man's singing, they shout "Bravo!" If they love a lady's singing, they shout "Brava!"

BRAVA, Leona. BRAVA!

Leona, second from left, and the Oklahoma Hall of Fame Class of 2004.

So you want to be an opera singer? Top 10 tips for young people.

1.   Don't be in a hurry! Opera singing is for adults. Just like an athlete, your body must be fully developed with the strength and stamina of an adult for your voice to handle the stress of singing in this style. Singing opera when you're too young can cause permanent damage to your voice. Be smart!

2.   Learn an instrument! Opera singers who have big, beautiful voices but can't read music are pretty much useless. The best instruments to study include piano or string instruments such as the violin, but any orchestral instrument will be beneficial. Take lessons—and practice!

3.   Sing in a healthy, non-stressful way. Audition for a reputable children's choir in your community. If there isn't one, sing in your school chorus or in a church youth choir.

4.   Listen to good music—all kinds, not just whatever your friends are listening to. Resources like your public library or the YouTube website will provide recordings and videos of famous classical singers. The more you listen to opera singers, the more accustomed you will become to the sound of a trained voice.

5.   Students from the age of 12 and above should consider private instruction with a reputable voice instructor. Be choosy about an instructor! Well-qualified voice teachers charge a reasonable fee for lessons and have at least a Master's degree in voice.

6.   Become interested in all art forms to be a well-rounded artist. Visit museums, see a ballet, attend theatrical productions. Opera is an art form that incorporates history, visual art, dance and acting skills; knowledge of the arts makes you a better opera singer.

7.   Audition for plays or musicals, whether community productions or school plays.

8.   Read! Read biographies, novels, poetry and books of all varieties.

9.   If your choral director or voice teachers find that you have vocal talent, plan on studying music at the college level. Education is the key to success in any field, and music performance is no different.

10. Be aware that the road to a career as an opera singer is difficult. Even the brightest stars experience disappointment, frustration and failure before achieving success. Those who make it have a true dedication to music and the perseverance to work toward their goals.

Credit: Dr. Glenn Winters, Community Outreach Music Director for Virginia Opera and composer of six children's operas.

The Mitchell Children

Hulon Jr.
Ramona
Thelma
Leon
Barbara
Palmor
James
Jefferson
William
Leona
Oliver
Milton
Marvin
Byron
Clifford

Pastor Mitchell often told his wife that they did not need an automatic dishwasher. They already had fifteen dishwashers.

Fun Facts

Leona's father built a separate section of their house just for her 10 brothers.

Leona's mother always played a few notes on the piano as she passed it on her way to the kitchen.

Leona's mother said Leona was very affectionate.

Leona would always call home if she was going to be late.

Sometimes Leona sang two roles in college operas.

Leona tried out and made the Oklahoma City University cheer squad, but her voice professor said she would have to resign before she ruined her voice.

Leona has worked as a secretary, sales clerk, and telephone operator.

In 1973, Leona won a $10,000 grant from Opera America.

When Leona first started traveling, she did not have money for hotels. But she always had a brother or sister living nearby.

Mrs. Priebe was afraid of flying, but Leona talked her into coming to the New York Metropolitan Opera. When she saw Leona perform, she cried all night.

Leona was often booked for performances five years in advance.

Glossary

Ambassador	person who represents their state or country while traveling away from home
Ancient pyramids	built in Egypt more than 2,000 years ago. Square bottom with triangle sides
Aria	a song from an opera
Audition	to show what you can do by giving a short performance
Baton	a thin stick a conductor uses to show musicians how to play a song
Conductor	the person who stands in front of the musicians with a baton
Debut	the first time something happens
Diplomat	a person who represents their country's government
Diction	to talk or sing clearly
Director	the person who decides how actors and actresses should play their role
Gospel	music based on Christian beliefs
Linguist	a person who speaks many languages
Lyric soprano	a soprano who can sing long high phrases, usually plays the role of a young person
Orchestra	a group of musicians
Pharaohs	the people who ruled in Egypt long ago
Professional	a person with special training and gets paid for what they do
Scholarship	an amount of money given to a person to attend college
Soprano	a female's high singing voice
Spinto soprano	a soprano with a high, deep, and dramatic voice
Voice coach	a music teacher who helps a person sing better

Timeline

1949	Born in Enid, Oklahoma
1971	Graduated from Oklahoma City University
1973	Debuted in *Carmen* with the San Francisco Opera
1974	European debut in Barcelona, Spain
1975	Debuted in *Carmen* with the New York City Opera
1975	Recorded *Porgy and Bess*
1976	Performed for President Gerald Ford
1978	Performed for President Jimmy Carter
1979	Married Elmer Coles Bush, III (one son—Elmer Coles Bush, IV)
1979	Received Honorary Doctorate Degree from Oklahoma City University
1983	Inducted into Oklahoma Women's Hall of Fame
2001	Inducted into Oklahoma Music Hall of Fame
2003	Performed at Oklahoma Governor Brad Henry's Inauguration
2004	Named Oklahoma's Cultural Ambassador
2004	Inducted into Oklahoma Hall of Fame
2005	Rode on the Oklahoma Rising Float in New York City for the 79th Annual Macy's Thanksgiving Day Parade.
2015	Sang the state song, "Oklahoma", at Oklahoma Governor Mary Fallin's inauguration

To Learn More about the World of Opera

A glossary of terms	http://www.sdopera.com/Operapaedia/Glossary
A summary of operas	http://www.sdopera.com/Operapaedia
Types of opera voices	http://www.sdopera.com/Operapaedia/Glossary/voice
When to Laugh or Clap	http://dallasopera.org/learn/faq
Opera or musical	http://dallasopera.org/learn/opera101

Listen to Opera Online

Leona singing *Porgy and Bess*

http://www.youtube.com/watch?v=H9HdVmBu5zg
http://www.youtube.com/watch?v=yRZkjrlju6M

Leona singing *Carmen*

https://www.youtube.com/watch?v=fCF-qTSQZFs

Leona and one of The Three Tenors, Luciano Pavarotti singing *Tosca*.

https://www.youtube.com/watch?v=yPbDQIOIA9k

Leona singing *Aida*

http://www.youtube.com/watch?v=H6I6ocjaqrw

Places to Visit

Leona Mitchell Southern Heights Heritage Center and Museum
616 Leona Mitchell Boulevard
Enid, Oklahoma 73701
580-237-6989
http://www.leonamitchellsouthernheightsindianmuseum.org/

Cimarron Opera
555 South University Boulevard
Norman, Oklahoma 73069
405-364-8962
http://cimarronopera.org/

Tulsa Youth Opera
Chapman Music Hall
110 East 2nd Street
Tulsa, Oklahoma 74103
918-582-4035
www.tulsaopera.com

**Oklahoma Hall of Fame
at the Gaylord-Pickens Museum**
1400 Classen Drive
Oklahoma City, Oklahoma 73106
OklahomaHOF.com

Teachers' Guides for the I AM OKLAHOMA CHILDREN'S SERIES available at OklahomaHOF.com under the Education tab.

Places to Visit, continued

Opera in the Ozarks at Inspiration Point
16311 Highway 62 West
Eureka Springs, Arkansas 72632
479-253-8595
www.opera.org

Opera in the Ozarks photos courtesy David Bell.

Located in the Ozark Mountains in northwest Arkansas, Inspiration Point sits 600 feet about the White River. It is a summer music camp for aspiring opera singers. Students come from all over the United States.

Leona attended the camp after her first year of college.

Sometimes the students present a traveling show to the nearby cities. It is called the Studio Arts Program. They perform in schools, libraries, and community auditoriums. The photographs show the students who sang in the opera, *Cinderella*. David Ward arranged and produced it. David used pieces of several *Cinderella* operas to make a 55-minute version. He translated it into English. The students traveled to Eureka Springs, Fayetteville, and Bentonville. They are all cities in Arkansas. Young students and adults loved watching the opera.

Index

Author Biography

Gwendolyn Hooks is the author of many books for children including *Porpoises in Peril* and The Pet Club Stories series. She also has a nonfiction science series about food webs. Gwendolyn has written for a South Korean publisher and an English publisher. Some of her books have been translated into Spanish and one is in French.

She taught seventh grade math until the day she realized she wanted to write for children. She says, "It's a super cool job!" She writes in her home office. But for inspiration, Gwendolyn walks in her neighborhood park. She hopes a squirrel will drop an acorn on her head that will explode into a new book idea. If that doesn't work, she explores the amazing museums in Oklahoma. Gwendolyn has three adult children. She lives in Oklahoma City with her husband.

To learn more about Gwendolyn, visit gwendolynhooks.com and oklahomachildrensauthors.com.